Jake's Dream

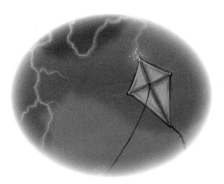

by Ronda Greenberg

illustrated by Eric Reese

PEARSON

Scott
Foresman

Editorial Offices: Glenview, Illinois • Parsippany, New Jersey • New York, New York
Sales Offices: Needham, Massachusetts • Duluth, Georgia • Glenview, Illinois
Coppell, Texas • Ontario, California • Mesa, Arizona

ISBN: 0-328-13231-4

7 8 9 10 V010 14 13 12 11 10 09 08

Jake slouched under the tree in his backyard. He was definitely having a bad day. His assignment was to come up with an idea for the "Great Ideas Fair" at his school. But Jake couldn't think of a good idea, let alone a great one.

Meanwhile, his little sister Susan was kicking dirt around the yard and moaning.

"I'm bored," she said. "Everything is boring."

Jake did not want to listen to Susan complain, so he went up to his room and started to think about a movie he saw in school. It was about Benjamin Franklin who lived a long time ago. Ben Franklin invented many important things and had many good ideas. Jake wished Ben Franklin were around to help him with an idea right now.

But Jake was so tired from thinking that he fell asleep and began to dream.

In his dream, Jake went down to his mailbox where he found a letter from, of all people, Ben Franklin!

Dear Jake,

I heard you were having a problem coming up with a clever idea for your Great Ideas Fair. I hate to see you feeling so bad, so I thought I would write you a letter. Maybe if I tell you about some of the things I've done, it will help you get an idea of your own.

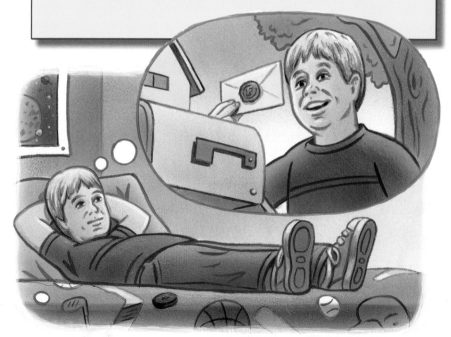

You might remember that I loved inventing contraptions. One of my all-time favorite inventions is what you now call a *grabber*. I came up with the idea one day while trying to reach a book from a high shelf in my library.

I took a wooden pole and put a kind of claw at the end. The claw helped grab the book off the shelf. I called it the *long arm*. It was a simple idea that worked quite well.

I liked inventing things, but I also wanted to understand nature and the world around me, like lightning. Back in my time, nobody knew what lightning was.

I thought that lightning might have something to do with electricity. As you know, electricity is a type of energy. It makes the lights in your house go on and your TV work.

So on a stormy day, I tied a piece of pointed metal to my kite. Then I tied a key to the bottom of the kite string. I let my kite sail off into the wild dark sky.

The sky was full of thunder and lightning. I could feel the energy in the air. The energy from the lightning went all the way down the kite string to

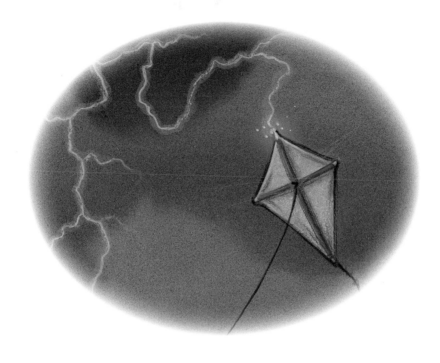

the key. When I touched the key, there was a spark! The spark proved that lightning was electricity.

Electricity can be very dangerous, and lightning can kill people. I was lucky I wasn't hurt. Never try experiments with electricity without a grown-up around.

Jake, I hope you are enjoying reading my letter so far. As for me, I love to read—all kinds of books.

I wanted everyone to have books to read. But in my time, books cost a lot of money. Only very rich people could buy them. That seemed unfair. So, some friends and I put our money together and bought books.

We opened a library so that everyone could borrow books to read. It was the very first lending library in America!

Well, Jake, it's time for me to say good-bye, but I hope this letter has helped you. I believe you are a fine and clever boy, and I feel sure that you will not have much trouble coming up with a good idea.

Best of luck,
Benjamin Franklin

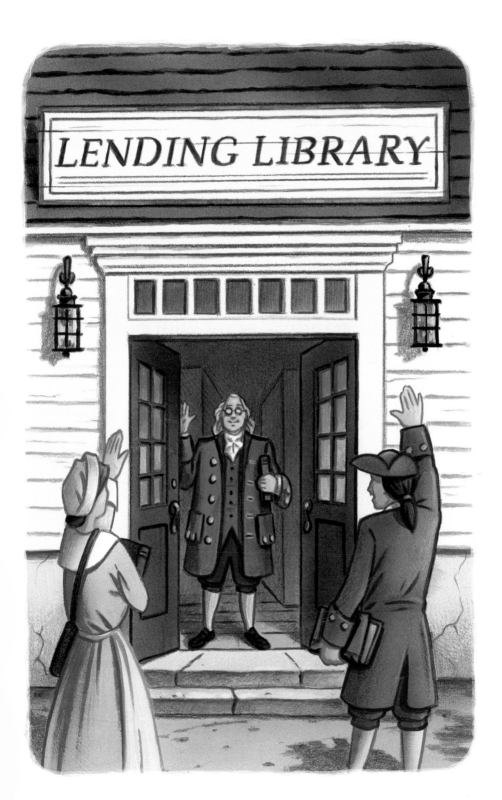

In his dream, Jake refolded the letter and put it in his pocket. Then, he heard shouting. The shouting became louder and louder still. It woke him up!

Jake peered out the window. The shouting was coming from his sister Susan.

"All my toys are boring! I want new ones! I want an airplane for my doll to fly. I want a purple pony with pink hair. Please!" cried Susan.

"We can't buy new toys whenever you want them," said Mom. "Toys are expensive. Play with the ones you already have."

"I wish Susan would be quiet," Jake thought. "I still need to come up with an idea."

Jake thought Ben Franklin certainly had come up with a lot of interesting ideas. He invented a grabber, experimented with lightning, and even started a lending library.

Again, Jake looked out the window to the yard where Susan was still fussing. He thought again about Ben Franklin's ideas. Suddenly, he knew what to do!

"I'll start a library, just like Ben Franklin," said Jake. "Only it will be a *toy* library. Kids can bring in their toys and trade them for different toys! It will be like having a new toy all the time, and it won't cost a cent."

His mother said, "Jake, this is an all-time great idea! You should enter the idea in the Great Ideas Fair. It's sure to make everyone happy!"

That is exactly what Jake did.

Connection Head

Ben Franklin invented swim fins, a musical instrument called the armonica, and a special kind of eyeglasses called bifocals, as well as many other things.

In the letter to Jake, you read that Ben Franklin loved books. He also printed books. His first job was as a book printer. Later he owned his own print shop.

Ben Franklin helped many people in his day. He started the fire department in his city. He helped find ways to deliver mail more quickly. He was a man who believed in solving problems. What problems would you like to solve?

One of Ben Franklin's inventions was bifocals.